921
YEA

Ayres, Carter M.

Chuck Yeager.

$13.50

3319700024476

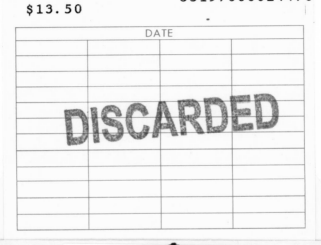

Chuck Yeager

THE ACHIEVERS

Chuck Yeager
Fighter Pilot

Carter M. Ayres

Lerner Publications Company ▪ Minneapolis

ACKNOWLEDGMENTS: The photographs are reproduced through the courtesy of: pp. 1, 2, 9, 11, 12, 15, 20, 22, 24, 29, 30, 35, 42, 43, 46, National Air and Space Museum, Smithsonian Institution; p. 7, Don Berliner; p. 18, Lockheed Aircraft Corporation; pp. 19, 44, United States Air Force; pp. 27, 31, 48, AP/Wide World Photos; pp. 34, 39, National Aeronautics and Space Administration; pp. 40, 41, Bettmann Newsphotos. Front cover: United States Air Force. Back cover: United States Air Force (left); National Air and Space Museum, Smithsonian Institution (right).

For their assistance in the preparation of this book, the author wishes to thank Mary Anne Thompson and Bob Dreesen, National Air and Space Museum, Washington, DC; Chet and Judith Bowie, Kensington, Maryland; and Col. Robert E. Fritsch, WIANG (Ret.), Sun Prairie, WI. The author also wishes to acknowledge the following bibliographic sources: *Across the High Frontier* by William Lundgren, *The Right Stuff* by Tom Wolfe, and *Yeager* by General Chuck Yeager and Leo Janos.

For Gordon Wells, with deep appreciation

LIBRARY OF CONGRESS CATALOGING-IN-PUBLICATION DATA

Ayres, Carter M.
  Chuck Yeager, fighter pilot.

  (The Achievers)
  Summary: Describes the life of the West Virginia boy who won a place in the history of aviation as the first pilot to fly through the sound barrier.
    1. Yeager, Chuck, 1923-   —Juvenile literature. 2. Air pilots—United States—Biography—Juvenile literature. [1. Yeager, Chuck, 1923-   . 2. Air pilots] I. Title. II. Series.
  TL650.Y4A97   1988   623.74'6048'0924 [B] [92]   87-3732
  ISBN 0-8225-0483-9 (lib.bdg.)

Manufactured in the United States of America

International Standard Book Number: 0-8225-0483-9
Library of Congress Catalog Card Number: 87-3732

2   3   4   5   6   7   8   9   10   96   95   94   93   92   91   90   89   88

CHUCK YEAGER: FIGHTER PILOT

On October 14, 1947, Charles E. "Chuck" Yeager won a place in the history of aviation as the pilot who first flew through the sonic "barrier" to winged flight. This retired United States Air Force general, who is considered one of America's most accomplished pilots, was born on February 13, 1923, and grew up in a rural setting with almost no exposure to airplanes of any sort. His father, Albert Hal Yeager, was a gas driller in the mountains of West Virginia, and Chuck's early years were, in many ways, unremarkable. He did well enough in school, but he was not at the top of his class. He played trombone with his high school band, and he enjoyed math. Chuck didn't care much for English or history, however, and one of his teachers said he was a bit "slow." To her, Charlie Yeager was quite ordinary, with no special talents.

Unlike the people with whom he would later work—people like Neil Armstrong, who would one day walk on the moon—Chuck Yeager did not spend his boyhood making model airplanes and learning all he could about them. Instead, he fished the Mud River for bass, hunted wild game with his .22-caliber rifle, or, sometimes, just wandered in the woods. Occasionally, he would hear an airplane overhead, but that was his only acquaintance with flying as there was no airport near his hometown of Hamlin.

Chuck's mother, Susie Mae Yeager, instilled the importance of personal responsibility in her children while they were still young. When they returned from walking in the hills, Chuck and his older brother, Roy, had chores to do, including milking and feeding the few cows the family owned. The Yeagers lived simply, but they were close. They cared a great deal about each other and shared what they had.

During high school, Chuck had an after-school job in Hamlin cleaning a photographer's studio. To him, it was work with no future, and he soon began to grow restless. As his dad had often said, small towns did not have many opportunities for young men. When Chuck heard talk about the war that had begun in Europe, his thoughts turned to flying, and, after graduating from high school in 1941, he enlisted in the United States Army Air Force. Eighteen-year-old Chuck knew nothing about flying, but he decided he wanted to learn. Here was an opportunity for a career and a future as a fighter pilot.

Yeager, however, didn't fly an airplane for months after he began his training. First came basic training at Ellington Field in Texas, where the emphasis was on military drill and discipline. Next, he studied aircraft mechanics at Mather Field in California, and then he worked at Moffett Field as a crew chief with AT-6's. After the United States entered World War II on December 7, 1941, Yeager transferred to Victorville Air Base in California, where he worked as a crew chief with AT-11's. Here he was promoted to the rank of private first class and eventually to corporal.

AT-6 trainers gave Yeager his first opportunity to learn about aircraft carriers, instruments, and in-flight handling.

As Yeager worked in and around airplanes, he learned a great deal about how they worked. Whenever he had time, he would sit inside the parked trainer planes and think about flying them. Then in August of 1942, Yeager went to Ryan School of Aeronautics in Hemet, California, for flight training.

The Ryan PT-21 training plane was Yeager's introduction to becoming a pilot. Once airborne, he had to learn how to coordinate the aircraft's control surfaces—the ailerons that banked the wings, the rudder that pushed the nose around, and the elevators that pulled the nose up —so he could make smooth turns. When making landing approaches, he discovered the airplane would glide further if he let the nose drop. On landing, he was taught to hold the aircraft off the runway as long as possible—an idea that at first went against all of his instincts. Yeager found that flying demanded concentration, coordination, and the mastering of many new skills.

The student pilot also had to learn about weather systems and how to navigate in varied flying conditions. Wind blowing past a line of hangars could make an aircraft jump around on its final approach, and a warm front could reduce visibility to almost nothing. A cold front very often produced thunderstorms and air currents that could tear an airplane to shreds. Chuck also had to learn how to use a compass for navigation and to understand the effects of wind speed and direction while flying. This, in turn, required the ability to read weather reports and

Student pilots in PT-21 training planes learn to fly in close formation.

maps. By now, Yeager knew he wanted to be a pilot, so he studied hard. As he gained experience, he began to feel more self-confident in the air.

Yeager became even more fascinated with aviation when he was transferred to Luke Field near Phoenix for advanced flight training in January of 1943. While shaky at first, his confidence grew rapidly as he learned formation flying, crosswind landings, aerobatics, and gunnery. To

Yeager, this was real flying! His skills as a pilot began to be noticed, and he became so good that his instructor recommended him for further training as a fighter pilot.

From the time he began flying, Yeager had wanted to be a fighter pilot. Now he was one of an elite group of army air force flight officers assigned to the 363rd Flying Squadron, flying P-39's out of Tonopah, Nevada. It was while he was flying with the squadron that Yeager met 18-year-old Glennis Dickhouse at a USO office in Oroville, California. Chuck was immediately attracted to her, but they had only a few months together before having to rely on letters to keep in touch.

As the squadron members became more and more skilled as fighter pilots, they began to look ahead to combat in the skies over Europe. When they were transferred to England to join the Allied 8th Air Force, they had to familiarize themselves with the new P-51 Mustang, the long-range fighter aircraft in which they would soon test their skills against the Nazi *Luftwaffe*. In early 1944, they were assigned to their first mission.

Yeager had never flown under real combat conditions before, but he felt in control when he shot down his first Messerschmitt Me-109 over Berlin on March 4. The following day, on Yeager's eighth mission, three Focke-Wulf 190's swooped down on his plane, seemingly from nowhere. Despite quick action, Yeager could not avoid the surprise attack. His plane was hit and caught on fire, and Yeager had to bail out over the south of France.

Chuck Yeager considered the North American P-51 Mustang to be the finest fighter plane in use during World War II.

The Focke-Wulf 190, however, was a worthy match for the P-51.

Yeager's foe followed his fall but was attacked by another plane from Yeager's squadron. A passing woodcutter brought a French farmer working with the Resistance to rescue Yeager, and he hid him in his barn. While in hiding, Yeager narrowly escaped detection by the Nazi soldiers patrolling the area. A week later, Yeager, disguised as a French peasant to escape detection, began traveling across the French countryside into Spain. In unfamiliar and enemy-occupied country, he constantly feared being discovered and shot.

In his P-51 fighter, Yeager had his skills as a pilot and his .50-caliber machine guns to protect him, but now he had to depend solely on his wits and his ability to control his fear. As he approached the Pyrenees Mountains along the Spanish border, German soldiers fired on Yeager and on the three other pilots who were escaping with him. One of the pilots was badly wounded in the leg, and Yeager carried him over the mountains to safety. For his courage and for saving his comrade's life, Yeager received the Bronze Star "for heroism displayed while in enemy-occupied Continental Europe." Flight Officer Yeager was also made a commissioned officer in the army air force and promoted to the rank of captain.

Following his escape, Yeager returned to England, more eager than ever to be back in combat. But his career as a fighter pilot almost ended when the Allied Expeditionary Forces in London told him he could no longer fly because if the Nazis ever caught him, he would be forced to tell what he knew about the work of the French Resistance. Yeager's enthusiasm for flying, however, made him determined to be reassigned to his old squadron. Fortunately, the policy regarding men who had escaped the Germans was changed after the June 6, 1944, Allied invasion of Europe, so Yeager was able to return to active combat duty. In the months since he had been shot down, Yeager had developed a full-fledged hatred for the Nazis. He wanted to go back and blast them out of the sky.

The risks of combat created an enduring bond among the pilots in Yeager's squadron, and, after returning from a mission, they would always talk about their encounters with Nazi planes: the dives they had made at 500 miles an hour, the way their P-51's had hammered the enemy with machine-gun fire, the turns that had pulled them back into their seats with four times the force of gravity. On one occasion, Yeager attacked plane after plane, shooting down one after the other. "Came up on them like a covey of quails," he would say later. "Shot one down, then went on to the next." His method was to "get up about 100 feet behind, then hammer them. Drop down a little and hammer them underneath. Maybe kick a little rudder and slide off the side and hammer them there. That way the pieces falling off go right on by." The squadron also suffered many losses, as one of every two men was eventually killed in action.

By the time Yeager returned to the United States in February of 1945, he had earned a number of distinguished military citations. In addition to his Bronze Star, he was awarded the Silver Star, the Distinguished Flying Cross, the Air Medal, the Purple Heart, and the Presidential Unit Citation for his courageous contribution to the Allied victory in Europe. During his 64 combat missions over occupied Europe, he had flown 270 combat hours and was officially credited with shooting down 11.5 enemy aircraft. The "half" came when his wingman joined in an attack. "Well, we shared airplanes, see. I hammered a guy pretty good, and then I let my wingman shoot at him so he could finally learn how, so I shared it with him," Yeager stated.

On February 26, 1945, Yeager married Glennis Faye Dickhouse, the young woman he had met during his training days in California. For Chuck and Glennis—and for the United States—the end of World War II signaled a new beginning filled with both problems and promise.

For a short while after his return, Yeager spent a relatively unrewarding time at Perrin Field in Texas as a flight instructor. His love of dogfighting and aerobatics was lost on his students, so Yeager soon transferred to the Fighter Test Branch, Flight Test Division, at Wright Field near Dayton, Ohio. As a maintenance officer there, he was involved in testing the new jet-powered P-80 Shooting Star and P-84 Thunderjet fighters. He also evaluated the

While a maintenance officer at Wright Field, Yeager often flew the Lockheed P-80 Shooting Star in air shows.

German and Japanese fighter aircraft that had been recovered after the war. For Yeager, flight testing was much more rewarding than teaching. It also gave him the chance to participate in a new program that would test a pilot's skills as much as combat. Yeager and many other pilots in the flight test division submitted their applications for the project.

In December of 1943, representatives from the U.S. Army and the U.S. Navy had joined with the National Advisory Committee for Aeronautics (NACA)—later known as NASA, the National Aeronautics and Space Administration—and the Bell Aircraft Corporation to design and build a new research aircraft. The plane was to be a high-speed laboratory for exploring aircraft performance up to and exceeding the speed of sound. Bell engineers Robert Woods and Robert Stanley would create the design, and Lawrence D. Bell, the corporation's president, would oversee the project. Their goal was to provide information to use in designing improved military jet fighters, and, by late 1944, the group was preparing to build the Bell X-1.

Before production of supersonic fighter aircraft could begin, the experimental X-1 would be used to solve many problems. One was the intense buffeting suffered by conventional military aircraft when they were flown near the speed of sound. The deadly *buffeting,* or severe shaking, which began as the aircraft entered the so-called transonic range, created a real danger for both pilot and plane, and pilots had died while making high-speed power dives near the speed of sound. Transonic speeds were reached just before Mach 1, the scientific name for sonic flight, or the speed of sound. This was the speed the Bell engineers would explore with the X-1 so that the problems encountered there could eventually be understood and, as a result, eliminated.

At the time of the development of the X-1, it was known that the buffeting was created because air flowing around a plane travels at different rates of speed around different parts of the aircraft. Scientists and engineers feared that as pilots pushed closer to the speed of sound, the buffeting would become worse and worse, until the airplane would be torn apart right before reaching Mach 1. Attempting to fly at Mach 1 was, therefore, considered highly risky—and even impossible. To most people, Mach 1 stood as a solid brick wall in the sky.

In 1946 and 1947, when Yeager was relatively new to the flight test division, it was hard for him to know just how good he was in the air. He was a class-A combat pilot, but he knew relatively little about engineering and rocket-powered test aircraft such as the X-1. Colonel Albert Boyd, the commanding officer of the division, noticed a number of unique qualities in the young aviator, however. Yeager's flying was always precise, and he valued safety. He was calm under pressure and always left himself a way out of danger when taking calculated risks in the air.

Colonel Boyd saw these qualities and Yeager's mechanical skills as proof of his potential for becoming an

In 1947, Yeager's commanding officer, Colonel Albert Boyd, set an air speed record of 623.8 miles per hour in his P-80 Shooting Star, the *Racey.*

outstanding experimental test pilot. He assigned Yeager to the X-1 project as pilot and Captain Robert Hoover as Yeager's alternate. Captain Jackie Ridley would be the project engineer. Together these three men would explore flight in the transonic range, gradually increasing their speed until—if all went well—they exceeded the speed of sound. The X-1 was picked up in Buffalo, New York, and transported by a B-29 to Muroc Air Base, California, where the testing was scheduled to take place.

The X-1 was totally experimental, totally unique—and built for speed! It was powered by four rocket engines, each generating 1,500 pounds of thrust. With no throttle for increasing or reducing its power, the aircraft would be

Colonel Albert Boyd buckles on his parachute prior to his record-breaking flight in the P-80.

The Bell X-1 rocket-powered research plane was designed to resemble a .50-caliber bullet.

flown at one of four settings—25, 50, 75 or 100 percent of full power. It was also extremely strong and built to withstand loads of up to 18 times the force of gravity, which would prevent it from breaking during the buffeting while flying at transonic speeds. The X-1's wing, only three inches thick, had been especially designed to reduce buffeting, as had the horizontal stabilizer located high on its tail. Lacking any real information about how a supersonic plane should be designed, the Bell engineers had used common sense and had designed the X-1 like a high-velocity bullet to enable it to pass through the transonic range and continue to fly beyond Mach 1.

Although the engineers had reduced the chances of buffeting and structural failure as much as possible, the X-1 was still a dangerous aircraft to fly. Its four rocket engines were fueled by liquid oxygen and alcohol, and, if a single part in the fuel system were to fail, the result could easily be an on-board fire or a violent explosion that would demolish the aircraft and its pilot. These dangers were real, and fire broke out on more than one occasion after Yeager began taking the X-1 on powered flights.

Danger was part of the business of being an experimental test pilot, and Yeager knew that he had to face and effectively deal with it if he were to survive. As a pilot for the X-1 project, he perhaps lived with more dangers than any other pilot in the air force. While he respected the danger potential of the high-speed rocket, Yeager still kept a positive outlook. He belittled fear by calling it "apprehension," because he knew that fear could kill him if he ever allowed it to affect his flying. Yeager also studied the X-1's systems until he understood them thoroughly, and he learned how to plan ahead so that he would be ready for any emergency that came up. He believed he could live through the dangers of experimental test flights if he were careful.

The X-1 burned rocket fuel at an alarming rate. With all four engines firing, the aircraft used up 13,000 pounds of fuel in two and one-half minutes. To conserve more fuel for high-speed flying, the aircraft's designers decided to launch the X-1 from the bomb bay of an airborne B-29

The Bell X-1, painted bright orange to improve visibility from the ground, was transported by a Boeing B-29 bomber and launched from its bomb bay.

bomber. At 5,000 feet, Yeager and Ridley moved back to the bomb bay in the belly of the bomber. Yeager then entered the X-1 by descending a ladder and swinging into the X-1's tiny cockpit. Once inside, he secured his equipment, including his parachute harness, seatbelt, oxygen mask, headset, and microphone. When Yeager was settled in, Ridley climbed down the ladder and helped Yeager secure the door, which hung from a cable. It was wearying work, with cold air blasting past the aircraft at 200 miles an hour. Adjusting the control stick to neutral, Yeager sat in darkness, waiting for the drop. Both behind and above him, chase planes jockeyed into position, ready to monitor his flight visually from the air.

Yeager's first flights in the X-1 were nonpowered. During those flights, he learned how the aircraft handled as he glided to a landing on Rogers Dry Lake, a hard, flat piece of California desert that was the Muroc Air Base's natural runway. Powered flights soon followed. Colonel Boyd now ordered Yeager to slowly and carefully explore the effect of transonic speeds on flight. As Yeager approached the speed of sound, beginning with Mach .82, the watchword was caution.

Although Yeager was cautious, he also experienced a great exhilaration whenever he flew the X-1. On his first powered flight, Yeager had been told only to fly past the tower and then land. Instead, he put the X-1 into a dive and descended from the B-29 at speeds reaching 500 miles an hour. After leveling off and silently passing the tower and "the brass"—the observers from the army air corps and Bell Aircraft—he ignited all four rocket engines and went straight up to 35,000 feet in a vertical climb. Ascending like a missile, he had to shut down all of his engines so he would not exceed Mach .85.

The challenge of the aerial frontier had completely captivated Yeager's energy and ambition, and he longed to push the X-1 to its limits. He had exceeded the maximum speed of the flight plan by Mach .03, and Colonel

Yeager climbs into the cockpit of the X-1. This aircraft and his earlier
P-51 warplane were favorites of his, and he named both of them
Glamorous Glennis.

Boyd was both enraged and jubilant at the young aviator's
challenge to the limits of manned flight. To Boyd and to
the Bell executives who were watching, it looked like
Yeager's attack on the sonic "barrier" might be successful.

The experience of flight at the speeds and altitudes
reached by the X-1 provided Yeager with a sense of real
satisfaction. Yeager flew because he liked to fly, and he
especially loved to fly the X-1. Yet, when things went
wrong with the aircraft, they went wrong fast. The X-1's
cabin filled with smoke a number of times, usually accom-

panied by engine trouble, and Yeager knew that one wrong move with a fire on board could blow both him and the X-1 to bits. Although Yeager knew he could handle an emergency such as an engine fire or ice on the windshield, he often had nightmares about trying to escape from a burning plane.

Even though her courage was equal to that of her husband, Yeager's dreams also scared his wife, Glennis. Chuck's test flights were harder on her, in a way, because she had no control over what Yeager did in the cockpit, and there was nothing to reassure her that her husband would return safely from a flight. And when he did arrive home safely, Glennis knew there would be another dangerous flight in a few days—or hours. The risks of test flights were similiar to the dangers of combat, and test pilots frequently died in the line of duty.

To share what was happening to him as he approached the speed of sound, Yeager would radio detailed information to Ridley while flying. At Mach .87, light buffeting began, and it increased markedly from Mach .88 to Mach .90. At Mach .90, Yeager started to lose his ability to move the plane's nose up and down with the control wheel—referred to as elevator effectiveness—and the loss of control continued to decrease up to Mach .94, when it virtually disappeared. After studying such ominous data, the project scientists and engineers told Yeager it would be extremely dangerous to go any faster. Yeager, however, believed that he would regain full control at faster speeds.

After all, bullets did not disintegrate when they traveled supersonically.

On October 14, 1947, the day that Yeager would attempt to fly beyond Mach 1.0, he radioed that he had regained elevator effectiveness at Mach .96. As he headed up with two of the rocket engines booming behind him, he continued to accelerate as he watched the needle of the machometer on his instrument panel move uneasily near the end of the scale. Yeager had reached the farthest edge of the transonic range, and the X-1 was flying better, not worse, than it had moments before. In the next instant, Yeager slid across the imaginary sonic barrier that people had long believed was real. Suddenly, he was flying at Mach 1.07 — faster than the sound the X-1 was making as it arced across the sky above the California desert.

After landing, Yeager was exhausted. When Glennis picked him up, he did not want to celebrate and only wanted to go home. Yeager's achievement was not made public for nearly eight months after his flight. But in the months and years that followed, he became a public figure in a way that few air force pilots ever had. His accomplishment was compared to those of the Wright brothers and Charles Lindbergh, and he made speaking appearances all over the world. Many people began thinking of Chuck Yeager as the best pilot in the United States Air Force. Yeager, however, felt he was not a better pilot than anyone else. Instead, he had been lucky enough to be the first to exceed the speed of sound.

Yeager talks to reporters at a 1949 press conference. By then, he had made more than 25 faster-than-sound flights, and the whole world knew about his achievement. The news of his first flight, however, had been kept secret for eight months.

As supersonic flights became routine, Yeager's responsibilities included testing a variety of experimental rockets besides the X-1. This increased the hazards of his work because it was difficult to get used to flying so many different kinds of aircraft. The constant newness of the systems and the varied flight characteristics of each made test flying a "nerve-wracking business," to use Jack Ridley's words. At no time were the risks greater than when Yeager was flying the Bell X-1A test aircraft.

Although the Bell X-1A was similar to the X-1 in many ways, it flew twice as fast, carried more fuel, and had a canopy for better pilot visibility. On December 12, 1953, Yeager's X-1A dropped from under the B-29 and began climbing to 80,000 feet. Beyond 45,000 feet, Yeager had all four engines firing behind him. Arcing over the top of the great curved path through the sky, Yeager reached 1,650 miles per hour—or Mach 2.5!

That flight, however, very nearly turned out to be Yeager's last. As the X-1A's fuel tanks emptied, the ship became lighter and less stable. When its fuel finally ran out and the rocket engines suddenly stopped burning, the aircraft slowed rapidly and started to tumble violently. Yeager lost control, and the X-1A became much like an empty tin can spinning end over end as it hurtled earthward.

Pressure up to 10 times the force of gravity smashed Yeager back and forth in the cockpit. He was badly bruised when his helmet crashed against the canopy's inner lining, and two oxygen bottles and fragments of plexiglass from the canopy flew in every direction. All Yeager could see were momentary glimpses of sky and desert. As the aircraft rushed toward earth at more than 1,000 feet per second, Yeager almost lost consciousness.

The X-1A descended through 34,000 feet. Its tumbling began to decrease, and it fell into a spin. Yeager had often put airplanes into spins as a test pilot, because, unlike the tumbling he had just experienced, spins could be controlled. Yeager forced his hands back to the control column. By the time the aircraft had reached 25,000 feet,

After a successful flight in the Bell X-1A rocket plane, Yeager is congratulated by Lawrence Bell, president of the Bell Corporation.

Yeager had stopped the spinning, increased his airspeed, and established a glide back toward Edwards Air Force Base (as Muroc was then called).

"The thing about doing research flying," Yeager would tell air force reporters many years later, "is that there may be 30 pilots to start out with, but then 28 of them bust their butts. You're left over and then you become a legend, not because you're good, but because you lived." Although Yeager always showed modesty when talking about his own flying, there was an element of truth to his words. He had been testing aircraft at Edwards for nine years and had flown almost every kind of military aircraft ever built. To continue as a test pilot would be inviting certain death.

Another experimental aircraft flown by Yeager at Edwards Air Force Base was the X-2 rocket-powered research plane.

In 1951, Yeager became the first pilot to fly a newer and faster version of the North American F-86 Sabre jet fighter, the F-86E, then the world's fastest airplane.

In remembering those years, Yeager could be proud of his contribution to better production aircraft design. "The military application of the testing data was very valuable," he said years later. "Because of what we learned about buffeting, the horizontal stabilizer of the Sabre jet, which was on the boards at that time, was redesigned. When Korea came along, we only lost one Sabre jet for every 12 MiGs....That's what had made all the difference in the Korean dogfights. Our pilots couldn't have been all that much better than theirs." Certainly, Yeager would always remember his days flying the Bell X-1. "It's still one of the prettiest little airplanes I've ever seen," he stated on a visit to the Smithsonian Air and Space Museum in Washington, DC, where *Glamorous Glennis* was displayed high above the museum's main entrance.

Although Yeager was proud of his work with the Flight Test Division, it had been grueling, and he now longed to once again fly with a squadron. In the three years that followed his 1954 departure from Edwards, Yeager served as commander of the 417th Fighter Squadron at Hahn Air Base in West Germany and at Toul-Rosieres Air Base in France. When he returned to the United States in 1957, Yeager was assigned to the 413th Fighter Wing at George Air Force Base in California, and, in 1958, was given command of the First Fighter Squadron of F-100 Super Sabres. As part of the Tactical Air Command, the squadron conducted a number of successful overseas assignments, including one to Moron Air Base in Spain. This was squadron flying as Yeager had always loved it, and he enjoyed leading a close-knit group of superior pilots.

In 1961, Yeager graduated from the War College at Maxwell Air Force Base in Montgomery, Alabama. Now a full colonel, he was assigned to be commandant of the United States Air Force Aerospace Research Pilots School (ARPS) at Edwards. Here Yeager would train the very best fighter pilots for work as test pilots and astronauts. Yeager's ARPS students enjoyed a reputation as the most elite group of pilots in the United States Air Force. Each year, only 48 students were chosen for training, and only a few of them would fly the proposed X-20, the space plane that would carry men and equipment into orbit around the earth, and back again.

Qualifying for the ARPS program was tough. Pilots had to be between 25 and 33 years of age and have at least 1,500 hours of logged flight time. Combat experience was common among the applicants, as were degrees in engineering and a strong background in differential calculus. Fitness was also essential. Eight instructors provided an intensive program of study in aerodynamics, physics, and mathematics, as well as flight training in a variety of aircraft. The goal of the program was to prepare future test pilots to accurately and reliably measure aircraft performance during flight. As Yeager had discovered years earlier, the work could be exacting, but also tedious, and very dangerous. Discipline and precision were still essential.

As commandant of the ARPS, Yeager resumed a regular schedule of test flying. One aircraft to be tested was the M-2, or the "flying bathtub," as it was called by the pilots. Yeager set about to evaluate the M-2 as a vehicle for training future astronauts in atmosphere reentry procedures. The motorless M-2 was hauled aloft on a tether and then released. It sank at 4,000 feet per minute. The M-2, an oddly shaped little ship, was designed to simulate the flight of a vehicle that would one day carry astronauts and their equipment between orbiting X-20's and the earth.

Yeager (seated) makes his first flight in NASA's M-2 lifting body research vehicle, a forerunner of the wingless aircraft that would allow astronauts to land on Earth following a space flight.

Nothing in Yeager's ARPS experience, however, could ever compare with his rides in the NF-104. A modified Lockheed Starfighter, the NF-104 had a rocket engine mounted over the jet engine's afterburner that was capable of generating 6,000 pounds of thrust. Together, the jet engine and the rocket engine would be able to put the aircraft over 100,000 feet up in the air. Like the M-2, the NF-104 was built to be a space mission simulator, but it had originally been designed as an airplane, not a rocket. As a military jet, it was a testy aircraft to fly, and no one knew how it would perform as a hybrid aircraft/space vehicle. Yeager jumped at the chance to see how the NF-104 would handle while teetering at the top of the flight's arc, just below the edge of space, where there was nothing but deep cold and virtually no atmosphere.

As in earlier rocket flights, Yeager's December 12, 1963, flight plan called for a big arcing curve that rose steeply and then fell off just as sharply. Toward the top of the arc, the NF-104 would no longer "fly." Instead, it would shoot upward under rocket power alone and then coast solely on momentum as it left the earth's atmosphere behind. On entering the atmosphere again, the pilot would have to activate the craft's hydrogen peroxide thrusters, which would push its nose down. This was crucial, for if the nose did not drop, the craft would spin and eventually crash on the desert floor.

The F-104 Starfighter, the first operational jet fighter to fly at Mach 2, was designed to give astronauts practical experience in high-aititude flight.

As with the X-1, Yeager increased the aircraft's performance one step at a time. First, he headed up to 60,000 feet using the jet engine and then, riding on rocket power, nudged the aircraft a little higher with each succeeding flight. On his fifth flight, Yeager reached 104,000 feet and, as called for in the flight plan, attempted to push the nose down to begin his descent.

Yeager heard the thrusters fire, but he was unable to drop the nose. At that altitude, there was just enough air rushing by to keep the nose pointed skyward. With all of its rocket fuel exhausted and its jet engine shut down, the NF-104 slowed, stalled, and then began to rotate rapidly while dropping like a cannonball. Unlike Yeager's brush with death in the X-1A, the NF-104 was in a flat spin—a deadly 9,000 feet-per-minute descent in which none of the ship's controls had any effect. It was too little speed—rather than too much—that prevented Yeager from regaining control of the aircraft. In short, the NF-104 had quit flying. If he were going to regain some flying speed and bring the aircraft back to Rogers Dry Lake in one piece, Yeager had no choice but to try to bring its nose back down.

Yeager tried to drop the nose by releasing the parachute stowed in the craft's tail for use as an air brake during landings. His plan worked. The tail jerked up, and the aircraft's nose pointed at the desert floor. Now if he could jettison, or throw away, the parachute, Yeager could regain speed—and maybe go fast enough to restart the jet engine. As he had hoped, the parachute billowed away behind the descending plane, and, all at once, the nose came back up! The control surfaces on the aircraft's tail were stuck at the position for climbing. With no engine, there was no hydraulic pressure, and Yeager could do nothing to move the controls.

Yeager had run out of options. He bent over, took hold of the ejection ring under his seat, and pulled. After falling 93,000 feet in his ship, Yeager was suddenly shot up and away from the hapless aircraft.

While Yeager had managed to eject safely, a new danger arose because the ejection seat that had blasted him away from the aircraft was now interfering with his escape. As Yeager's parachute began to open up, the remaining red-hot fuel from his ejection seat rocket touched his parachute lines and started them burning. Then, as his parachute filled with air, Yeager's descent suddenly slowed. The seat, still speeding earthward, slammed into his helmet, shattering the helmet's visor, and cutting the left side of Yeager's face near his eye. Even worse, rocket fuel from the underside of the seat oozed into his helmet, setting the left side of his head on fire.

The situation worsened rapidly. The fire burned a hole in Yeager's pressure suit, causing the suit's automatic oxygen system to feed pure oxygen to his face. The oxygen turned the fire into an inferno, and Yeager's head, neck, and helmet were engulfed in flames. He was in danger of losing his left eye, and, if he did not do something quickly, he would certainly lose his life.

Yeager had survived countless other situations by knowing how to respond to danger. Realizing the only way to put out the fire was to open his helmet's visor, Yeager pushed hard against the crushed plastic, severely burning his hand before the visor opened. The sudden rush of air put out the fire, and Yeager, burned and badly cut, fell to the desert floor. He was rushed to a hospital by helicopter, and his eye was saved because it had been covered by the crust of dried blood from his head wound. After weeks of treatment, Yeager was released and returned to active flight status. He had managed to escape any permanent disfigurement from the ordeal, and his eyesight remained a better-than-perfect 20/15.

When Yeager resumed his duties as the ARPS Commandant, he learned that the X-20 project would soon end. President Lyndon B. Johnson had decided to have NASA, and not the air force, continue the U.S. space program after the completion of the Mercury space missions. To Yeager, this was a mistake. "We could have been doing in the 1960s exactly what NASA did in 1981 with the Space Shuttle," he would say later. The Mercury, Gemini, and Apollo astronauts in the 1960s would not be doing any real flying as their capsules would be controlled primarily by ground-based controllers and computers. Yeager wanted none of that. He was, and always would be, a fighter pilot. Nothing Yeager could think of could ever justify sitting in a wingless capsule that had been test-flown by a monkey!

When NASA took over the U.S. space program, Neil Armstrong, the first human to walk on the moon, was one of six pilots chosen to continue the X-15 research project.

President Dwight D. Eisenhower awarded Harmon International trophies to Yeager and to Jacqueline Cochran for breaking speed records in the X-1A and the F-86, respectively. (On May 18, 1953, Cochran had become the first woman to break the sound barrier.)

Yeager left Edwards for the second time in 1966 and returned to conventional military flying—this time with the 405th Fighter Wing at Clark Air Base in the Philippines. While commanding the wing, he flew 127 missions over Vietnam. In 1968, he assumed command of the 4th Tactical Fighter Wing at Seymour Johnson Air Base in North Carolina and, the following year, was promoted to the rank of brigadier general, becoming vice commander of the 17th Air Force in West Germany. Two years later, he was appointed to be the U.S. defense representative to

Pakistan, and, in 1973, he became the director of aerospace safety for the U.S. Air Force Inspection and Safety Center at Norton Air Force Base in California. There Yeager was responsible for helping to prevent and reduce air accidents through safety education and inspection programs, accident investigation, and research into human factors affecting flight safety.

After 34 years of service, General Yeager officially retired from the U.S. Air Force in 1975. His pioneering contributions to aviation were recognized by a special medal given to him by President Gerald R. Ford. The award, created

Ten years after receiving an award from President Ford, Yeager was given the Presidential Medal of Freedom, the nation's highest civilian award, by President Ronald Reagan.

by the U.S. Congress as the noncombat equivalent of the Congressional Medal of Honor, was presented to General Yeager for being the first pilot to fly faster than sound. That memorable flight had first been recognized in 1948 when Yeager had received the MacKay Trophy for his outstanding work as a test pilot in the X-1 project. That same year, President Harry S. Truman also awarded Yeager, along with Lawrence Bell and John Stack of Bell Aircraft, the Collier Trophy for what the selection committee called "the greatest achievement since powered flight first began on the sands of Kitty Hawk."

President Harry S. Truman presents the Collier Trophy to Chuck Yeager and to Lawrence Bell (right).

The Northrop F-20 Tigershark was one of the excellent fighter aircraft that General Yeager flew after retiring from the U.S. Air Force.

To Yeager, retirement has not meant giving up flying, but rather the privilege of setting his own schedule. He has flown as a consultant for Northrop Corporation in the F-20 Tigershark and for McDonnell Douglas in the F-15 Eagle, and he has been an unpaid consultant to the Flight Test Center at Edwards Air Force Base. He has appeared in advertisements for various products and was a consultant for movie companies that needed his insights into military flight. In 1985, his autobiography, *Yeager*, written in the honest, down-to-earth language that has come to symbolize the test pilot, was published, and it would be followed by another book about the joys of flying, hunting, and fishing.

General Yeager's successes have evolved from his years of dedication to the air force, from his belief that he could break an imagined "barrier" to supersonic flight, and from his contributions to the development of modern fighter aircraft. Perhaps his greatest achievement, however, can be found in his attitude as a fighter pilot. Yeager loved to fly, and he decided while still a young man to become the best fighter pilot he could be. He was intent on success from his training days, and, as a result, his achievements have earned him recognition as one of the finest fighter and test pilots of all time.

Through the years, Glennis Yeager (shown seated with her husband in a Bell 47 helicopter) and their four children—Donald, Mickey, Sharon, and Susan—have given Chuck the security and support that has helped him to excel in a career filled with danger and uncertainty.

CHUCK YEAGER: FIGHTER PILOT

February 13, 1923	Charles Elwood Yeager is born in Myra, West Virginia.
September 12, 1941	Yeager enlists in the Army Air Corps. After completing basic training at Ellington Field in Texas, he becomes an aircraft mechanic at Mather Field in California.
August 1942	Yeager arrives at Ryan Field in Hemet, California, to attend ground and flight school.
January 1943	Yeager is transferred to Luke Field in Arizona for further training as a flight pilot.
March 1943	Yeager receives his wings and is assigned to the 363rd Fighter Squadron in Tonopah, Nevada.
June 1943	The 363rd moves to a temporary air base near Oroville, California, for two months. There Yeager meets Glennis Dickhouse, his future wife.
January 1944	Yeager and his squadron arrive at Leiston Air Base near Ipswich in England.
March 4, 1944	Yeager shoots down an ME-109 over Berlin. (Yeager had flown his first combat mission over Hamburg, Germany, in February but had not encountered any enemy planes.)
March 5, 1944	Ambushed by three Focke-Wulf 190's, Yeager is forced to parachute into Nazi-occupied France.
March 25-28, 1944	Yeager crosses the Pyrenees Mountains into Spain. After eight weeks in Spain and Gibraltar, he returns to England.
June 19, 1944	Yeager is reinstated as a fighter pilot.
October 12, 1944	While leading a squadron of P-51 Mustangs over Germany, Yeager shoots down five ME-109's and is awarded the Silver Star.
November 6, 1944	For shooting down an ME-262 jet fighter near a Nazi air base, Yeager receives the Distinguished Flying Cross. Two weeks later, he scores four victories when he and his squadron encounter a group of FW-190's near Berlin.
February 26, 1945	After returning to the United States, Yeager marries Glennis Dickhouse, and they move to Perrin Field in Texas.

This Week
MAGAZINE

The Sunday Star
WASHINGTON, D.C.
MAGAZINE SECTION • AUGUST 22 1948

Capt. Yeager's
X-1 takes off
from its B-29
mother ship

"I FLEW FASTER THAN SOUND"

For the first time Captain Charles E. Yeager (above) tells how he felt when he
gave his rocket plane the gun and wondered if it would disintegrate . . . Page 4

46

July 1945	Yeager transfers to Wright Field in Dayton, Ohio, and becomes a maintenance officer with the fighter test section of the flight test division.
November 1945	Colonel Albert Boyd, flight test division head, talks to Yeager about becoming a test pilot.
May 1947	Yeager is assigned to be principal pilot for the Bell X-1 research program.
August 1947	Yeager begins non-powered flights in the X-1.
October 14, 1947	On his ninth powered flight in the X-1, Yeager reaches Mach 1.07 at an altitude of 47,000 feet, breaking the sound barrier.
June 1948	The Air Corps officially confirms the X-1's supersonic flight. Yeager is awarded the MacKay Trophy and, several months later, receives the Collier Trophy.
January 5, 1949	Yeager makes the first supersonic flight in the X-1 from a full-power ground takeoff. Later that year, Colonel Boyd is promoted to general and moves the flight test division to Edwards Air Force Base in California.
December 12, 1953	Yeager flies at Mach 2.5 in the X-1A, breaking Scott Crossfield's Mach 2 record, but he loses control and narrowly avoids a fatal crash.
February 1954	Yeager test flies a captured MiG-15 in Okinawa, Japan. Several weeks later, he becomes commander of a fighter squadron flying F-86 Sabre jets from Hahn Air Base in West Germany.
April 1957	Yeager reports to George Air Force Base in California to command a squadron of F-100 Super Sabres.
June 1961	Colonel Yeager becomes commandant of the Aerospace Research Pilots School (ARPS) at Edwards Air Force Base.
December 12, 1963	After several successful test flights in the NF-104, Yeager must eject when the fighter goes into an unrecoverable flat spin.
July 1966	Following President Johnson's decision to reassign the air force's space program to NASA, Yeager becomes wing commander of the 405th Fighter Wing at Clark Air Base in the Philippines.
1968	Yeager is assigned to command the 4th Tactical Fighter Wing at Seymour Johnson Air Base in North Carolina.

47

1969	Yeager is promoted to brigadier general and is made vice commander of the 17th Air Force in West Germany.
December 1970	Yeager is reassigned to Pakistan as the U.S. defense representative.
March 1973	While serving at Norton Air Force Base in California, Yeager is appointed safety director for the U.S. Air Force.
March 1975	Yeager retires from the air force with more than 10,000 hours of flying time in 180 different types of military aircraft. He continues as a fighter test consultant for the air force and several aircraft manufacturers.
December 1976	Yeager receives a peacetime Congressional Medal of Honor.
May 1985	Yeager is awarded the Presidential Medal of Freedom.
July 1985	*Yeager: An Autobiography* is published in hardcover, and a paperback edition is issued in September 1986.

On December 17, 1986, Yeager set a new cross-country speed record when he flew this Piper Cheyenne 400LS from Edwards Air Force Base to North Carolina in five and one-half hours. The flight was part of the celebration at Kitty Hawk to commemorate the 83rd anniversary of the Wright Brothers first successful manned flight in 1903.